Fokkina McDonnell

Oversteps Books

First published in 2016 by   Oversteps Books Ltd
                                  6 Halwell House
                                  South Pool
                                  Nr Kingsbridge
                                  Devon
                                  TQ7 2RX
                                  UK

www.overstepsbooks.com

Copyright © 2016 Fokkina McDonnell
ISBN 978-1-906856-67-0

All rights reserved. No part of this book may be reproduced, stored in a retrieval system, or transmitted in any form, or by any means, electronic, mechanical, photocopying, recording or otherwise, or translated into any language, without prior written permission from Oversteps Books, except by a reviewer who may quote brief passages in a review.

The right of Fokkina McDonnell to be identified as the author of this work has been asserted by her in accordance with the Copyright, Designs and Patents Act 1988.

Printed in Great Britain by imprint digital, Devon

in memory of Linda Chase

Acknowledgements

With thanks to the editors of the following magazines and anthologies in which some of these poems first appeared: Orbis, The North, Magma, Erbacce, Little Mslexia, Presence, the Affectionate Punch, Pause, Best of Manchester Poets, vol 2, Best of Manchester Poets, vol 3 (Puppywolf), Traveller's Moon (Aural Images), Poems from the Readaround (Tarantula Press), The West in her Eye (Pyramid Press), The Ware Poets 14th Competition Anthology (Rockingham Press), For Rhino in a Shrinking World (The Poets Printery), Sweet Tongues (Commonword), Drifting down the Lane (Moon and Mountain).

Several poems were shortlisted or commended in competitions. *The Vienna of Sigmund Freud* won second prize in the 2012 Marple International Writing Competition. *Standing in for Utah* was awarded the RedPage Sonnet Prize in the 2012 Ware Poets Poetry Competition.

Special thanks to Ann and Peter Sansom, my fellow Chorlton and Writing School poets for inspiration, support and feedback. Thanks to Kathleen Kummer and Esther Köhler for their help in selecting which poems to include and to Helen Nicolson for proofreading the manuscript.

Contents

Part 1: Still casting a shadow
The Vienna of Sigmund Freud — 1
Separation — 2
Facts — 3
The Lido, Clifton — 4
Sunday morning — 5
Dublin Coddle — 6
Sunday evening — 7
Boxed — 8
St Nicolaas, 5 December 1957 — 9
On the town — 10
1962 — 11
Still casting a shadow — 12
At the clinic — 13
My father as a coat stand — 14
Friday evening — 15
Fairy tale — 16
Canteen — 17
Hat — 18
Outing — 19
Gardening — 20

Part 2: Trying
Trying — 21
Standing in for Utah — 22
Key notes — 23
Miniature French Suite — 24
Wooden — 26
The 'C' word — 27
In the town of Orihuela — 28
Morning — 29
Portrait of Johannes Wtenbogaert, — 30
Joan — 31
Satsumas — 32
Prelude and fugue — 33
On the beach — 34
Mishap — 35

Part 3: Another life
The hermit	36
Lost	37
Round and round	38
From Grassington, June	39
The ghosts have swapped houses	40
Flight of swallows, murmuration of starlings	41
Laughter	42
I want to be	43
On reaching his 102nd birthday	44
June rain	45
Festes patronals	46
Grandfather Lutz	47
If Bach had been a baker	48
Eel	49
Things I want you to bring when you next visit	50
Another life	51

The Vienna of Sigmund Freud
after Miroslav Holub

This is where they rein in Lipizzaner horses
and Schnitzler and Klimt shocked
and Hitler studied art.

And here an emporium reflects the cathedral.
Here they debate the merits of *Sachertorte*
and mature women wear hats with feathers.

This is where Freud analysed the disturbed
and the distressed sat in his red waiting room,
this museum with a clean flag and frosted glass.

And here the U-Bahn stations are without graffiti.
Here the shoppers whisper silently
and pain starts when sounds die.

Separation

A button has memories
of the coat it came from:
how blue wool smells in rain.

Maybe the small cork can still
sense the tightness of glass,
her curved fingers.

The trinket box lies empty.
Red velveteen finding
its own weight again.

Facts

Last year I got a Christmas card from Andrew Graham-Dixon
which he embroidered himself, or bought in Venice.

It is well-known that the card shops which went bust
were set up by Bill and Hillary to secure their pension.

Stravinsky kept a caged black bear in his music room.

These are the known facts: all of us keep
a black bear in a cage. Or black dogs on a lead.

Night follows day; a week has seven days.
But soon comes the week that will not end,

two black Sundays fighting it out.

The Lido, Clifton

It is dry this Monday morning.
I wonder what it's like swimming here
when it rains. Just then the drizzle starts,
a gently pulsating rhythm.

Bristol had the oldest open-air lido
in the country. Refurbished Grade II
it sits between the backs of offices.

The water is warm, kept at this
steady temperature. Floating on my back
I see the movement of clouds.

The following year my friend
would abandon me once I became ill,
but here we are drawing small ripples
in the water, each of us in our own lane.

Sunday morning

Frighten the eggs with cold water.
Do it quickly. A dog or a cat
for egg cup? You choose.
(The dog has a blue eye.
Sulphur yellow and spiteful
black make up the cat's
colour spectrum.) Just now
Joyce Carol Oates spoke
on *Private Passions* of her love
of Chopin and her interest
in boxing. Boxing has a history,
she said and, just like music,
you learn more from a replay.
It was an old city where that other
poet sat, coolly cracking
the egg of a fine Leghorn chicken.
Venice? Rhodes?
You tell me the title,
I'll give you the last line:
Surely we have ...
No! Don't start that again.

Dublin Coddle

Saturday supper is a savoury stew.
Sausages and slices of bacon.
Potatoes and onion supplanted
the oatmeal and leek. Enough stock

to barely cover, season to taste,
simmer slowly, let the liquid reduce.
Tears run down the steamy window.
Chopping parsley holds the pain.

One of us poured a steady Guinness;
the other already lost in the black
and salty taste of waiting.
Between us the open cookery book:

a small black and white picture,
North Earl Street, Dublin, 1904.
Blurred images of men in coats
and caps, horse-drawn cart, a sunny day.

A couple crosses the tramlines.
He carries bags in both hands.
She, to the right of him,
looks down to safely place her feet.

Sunday evening

Just leave them with a nurse on the ward.
I am eleven, the eldest, I can cycle, know
my way round town. There is only one
grocery shop open on Sundays,
opposite the Catholic school.

It's spring, I don't need a coat; if I'm quick,
I can stop to look at the bookshop on Broad Street.
Two large bottles of lemonade hang in bags
from the handlebars. The lights are coming on
as I go past the post office, railway station,
the Half Moon Park with small deer and goats.
Then it's a right turn towards the hospital.
People coming and going, some on crutches,
an empty ambulance by the door.

I've memorised the name of the ward, mumble
my instructions, but the nurse points down a corridor,
all bright and smelling of disinfectant.
Here is my grandmother, alone in a room,
resting in pale silk pyjamas my mother
bought; the second pair this week.
Ah, child she says, lifts her skull,
raises her hands, thin like hens' legs.

When I get home, crying, my mother is angry,
thinks I've dropped and broken those bottles.

Boxed

When I feel insecure, it's hard to see,
though I hear well, too well, that voice
that isn't mine, but mine.
I feel that my throat is a lock
and a lock needs a key
the key is a clock
and a clock loses time
that time is a fountain
and words are like frogs
that sit frozen under ice.

When I feel insecure, it's hard to read
though I hear well, too well that voice
that tells another story, not my story.
I feel that my gut is a basin
and a basin needs a spoon
that spoons are like owls
and owls are alone
and alone isn't safe
and a safe is
a bag, or a box, or a gag.

St Nicolaas, 5 December 1957

We're crowded in our dining room.
Grandmother has closed her face.
There's me in pyjamas, smiling.
I'm next to my father's father.
His heart will give out soon.
I've just been given a book:
animal stories with illustrations.

My brother too smiles, because
our mother isn't there.
She may be in the kitchen
or upstairs, ill, thinking
about walking out on us.
My father has taken this photo.
He too will have closed his face.

On the town

In the time it took to buy a birthday card, a special
80th birthday card, they had arrived in a long, black limousine,
jumped out, set fire to the hotel and released wicker
baskets. The flying baskets with wicker wings chopped
tops of trees, trees falling on traffic lights – chaos everywhere
and in the middle of it the small bronze statue.
A smiling woman holding doves covered in bird shit.
The wind howling, sirens crying like the end of the world had come.
And me and that card that had cost me £2.99 and nowhere
to buy stamps, no letter box to post it.

1962

Alexander Eduard (coppersmith
in the bible and *van Beinum,*
the famous conductor).
Our Irish setter had been given
the names of an unborn child.

A ward of six, our parents' daily
drive, forty minutes each way.
Neurologist, paralysis,
lumbar puncture, nausea.

Grandfather owned an electrical shop
(double-fronted on the main street);
gave my brother a beige-brown radio.

The specialist allowed our red
Irish setter to visit my brother,
celebrating his fourteenth birthday
in the academic hospital in Leiden.

Three months later he arrived home,
just in time for *St Nicolaas.*
My brother still limped and his crown
was marked by two scars at right angles,
the space between dipped and dented.
A few days later grandfather came
to take his radio back.

Still casting a shadow

Two unused scratch cards, with the faintest whiff of orange. Found on the floor of the Lowry, Salford after a performance of *The Love for Three Oranges* by Opera North. Purchased on eBay and donated by J Smith Esq.

*

Patina and Pathos. Today's lecture has been cancelled due (rest of notice torn off)

*

Scale drawings and recipe for three-tiered wedding cake: SEX, three wedding cakes in the shape of capital letters S, E and X, with red, white and blue marzipan. Decorated with 24 small edible doves and placed in a French sleigh bed made of walnut.

*

Spot the difference competition. Place your feet on the white X on the gallery floor for the best vantage point. Spot the differences between the wax model of an attendant and the live guard (seated). Put your form in the box.

*

Bronze box, still casting a shadow, with burnished lid, bronze hinges and clasp, key missing. Age of box indeterminate, size varies daily depending on the swelling and shrinking of contents.

At the clinic

Behind the grey gargoyles
soothing music sidles up to us
as we wait on pale beech seats.
(Furnished from legacies?)

Brassieres folded in blue plastic baskets
we eye each other for signs of decay,
pretending to read or doze.

Sagging, sunbronzed breasts
(no longer ours)
lie squarely splayed
between transparent plates
labelled Left and Right.
I cling on to the X-ray machine
like a baby baboon.

A tableau fired by neurons in the brain:
smiling surgeons, a chaperone.
Holding leaflets about wigs,
the breast nurse.
(Does she still have hers?)

Speaking slowly the consultant
inspects my face for cues of dismay.
The word sizzles in my head
like a yellow lemon sherbet:
Biopsy
Bye-op-see

Our companions collect us.
You construct a cautious smile
and examine me.
I feel okay
conceals
a sudden gust of envy.

My father as a coat stand

Taller and broader than he ever was,
freestanding, self-contained, pine.

For almost thirty years it has endured
wet raincoats, cold gusts from the open door.

Screwed in close, six curving handles,
like shiny antlers in autumn.

From that tight corner he has observed
the silence, shouting, tearful *adieux*.

And the wooden coat hangers my mother
used to beat my brother with.

Friday evening

He leaves work *early*,
walks *past* the pub,
unchaining habits,
dropping an old raincoat
into the Ribble.
Preston is still Preston,
magnificent failure.

If he can walk backwards
to the railway station,
he will catch himself
in the windows.
There is his 40th birthday,
never celebrated.
Here are the empty Sundays.
Swans, a football, his parents, baby sister.

Fairy tale
after Vasko Popa

Someone needs to go to
a deep cupboard in a dark room.
The others wait outside.

The first one becomes
a grandmother with a stoop.
Then someone else steals
her white lace cap her smile
her soft voice.
They go to lie still in a deep dark
bed in a cold room.

Then someone else walks a long
way through the wood, across
the saddled serpent under a cold
sheet of dark clouds.

That someone is dressed in crimson
already – it will save time.
The old one will rescue the red girl
but they will not have enough
bricks to finish the job.

After that someone else will get to be hungry
and someone will always be eaten.

Canteen

I find myself in a canteen,
a windowless oblong box
with grey furry walls.

Everyone in this canteen
is tall, thin, elegant,
all waiting neatly in line.

I see myself in this canteen,
my image reflected in my neighbour.
She too has curves.

I find myself in a canteen
of cutlery. I am a table spoon,
the knives are to my left.

Hat

That Saturday afternoon my father had been drinking with
the sales reps who'd driven in to collect their bonus and, of
course, being pleased with their bonus, they would have
bought my father a drink. My father, being generous and
liking his drink anyway, would have bought them a drink.
How the subject turned to hats, I don't know, but around
three, or three-thirty, my father came back home
and picked up my mother's hat, the one she would wear
to church the following day: a large peach-shaped,
red-wine-coloured, black-velvet-edged-bonbon-of-a-thing.
I watched my father put on this hat and leave the house.
I went out and followed him. The three sales reps stood
outside the café at the end of our road. With the disdain
of a Spanish matador, my father strode past them,
heading for the High Street.

Outing

My man, head down, was still reading a book
in his summer vacation (without pay).
His slight frown and that critical look.

So I proposed a day trip to the beach.
Relax, catch the sun, swim, play.
My man, head down, was still reading a book.

Under the sunshade, out of reach
he settled and rested. His slight frown
still stayed on his face. And that critical look.

I turned and tanned. Ate a peach
and thought that I might one day ...
My man, head down, was still reading a book.

I considered alternatives, each
in turn. There was nothing left to say.
His slight frown and that critical look.

But I lacked the strength to search
afresh and was fearful of swimming away.
My man, head down, was still reading a book.
His slight frown and that critical look.

Gardening

I tried growing cabbages,
but they got eaten
by the slugs.
So it's back to the clinic:
further tests,
more drugs.

If I had my time again,
they say,
I would not have kids.
I probably wouldn't
want to have them either,
if I could.

Trying

Trying not to be like
one who has gone before.
Allocated a slot
at the back of the queue:
a circle dancer with a club foot.

Striving to become
the symbol of perfection.
Dragging a tail
leaving tiny furrows
on the rough terrain.

Trying then to hide
in foreign places.
Archaic words spoken with a twang:
Qua, quorum, quota, quasi.

A cold place they tell me.
Quebec.

Standing in for Utah

They were given six weeks to pack and leave.
Round and oblong tables stowed in a van:
Hannaford the Butchers. Empty farms grieve
for cows, sheep taken by women and men.
Forty-six square miles behind Slapton Sands,
gravel, dunes, the flooded marshes of Lyme Bay.
A cold, still, grey hinterland that stands
in for Utah, the rehearsal for D-Day.
Three thousand people, animals, the year
before sent to live in another place.
Now American boys are sheltered here
and dodging live ammo with sudden grace.
    How small, the blue Heritage Coast dots on the map.
    Distant that April night when Start Bay was a trap.

Operation Tiger was the code name.
One tank landing ship keeled over and sank
in just six minutes, the wheelhouse aflame.
That boat spewed burning gasoline from its flank.
German *Schnellboote* fired the torpedo.
Rusted-up life boat tackle abandoned;
never told how to use life belts, below
seven hundred and forty-nine men drowned.
This is my ship and I am going back,
Lieutenant John Doyle, skipper, who turned,
against orders. Picked up shapes limp and black;
clinging on to charred life rafts, men who'd burned.
    Destiny is shaped by random things, often small:
      wrong frequencies, second chances, the place where you fall.

Key notes

It is a wet-leaved November,
the air full of birds, too many to count.
Small black bonfire flakes.

The key and the jewellery box have gone,
left like cats returning to the farmhouse
where they'd been born.

A small square patch on the piano,
the outline of that box: a sudden
sharp sound, a short piece of music.

Black dots rising, bar lines missing,
mostly rests for his hands to be still.
He wants those birds to be lost and swirling.

Miniature French Suite

Allemande

Do you mind if I borrow your man?
The old one with the beard that has
sparrows nesting in it. It's only
for the Open Gardens weekend.
He needs to wear something
beige-brown, corduroy and I'll
provide food. Tell him to wear
a cap or a sou'wester – something
to keep the fledglings dry.
He can hum to them. It might rain,
it could snow, warm boots.
Rameau or Telemann, I don't mind.

Sarabande

Rameau or Telemann, I don't mind.
A countertenor can't be that choosy.
A voice like that is a rare find
but keeping it alive and strong taxes
me and my agent, bless her.
She tells me to let go of worries
and fears. It's her domain to get
me engagements, book flights,
the new portrait and such.
She says a voice like mine is a horse,
that needs to be whispered to,
not broken in.

Gigue

I'm warming up in an empty church,
on a grey Sunday afternoon.
It's winter, the radiators gurgle,
the conductor is late.
I let my eyes wander in order
to keep my thoughts at rest
but now they take flight,
filling the gallery, the arches
and the painting of the old one
with the beard that has
sparrows nesting in it.

Wooden

my mother's lilac suit
matches the grey lining
of her coffin

The 'C' word

Only August and I have already heard
and seen the big 'C' word
on a number of occasions:
menus in pubs and posters on stations.

The first charity catalogues came in;
I swallowed and threw them straight in the bin.
Like birds fleeing from an earthquake,
friends are booking flights and a voice says I should make
my own cards this year.
Yes, the spectre of shopping days is here.
Bloody robins, three wise kings.
Bloody turkey, a stocking that sings.

There must be a self-help support group
meeting on Barbados or Guadeloupe
the day before St Stephen's Day.
To escape I am even willing to pray.

In the town of Orihuela

Day

The black sculpture of a priest
with a small girl by his side,
shining in the March sun.
The narrow streets are empty.
Oily puddles lie close to the walls
of the closed shops. It's Wednesday.
On the ring road the rumble of lorries.

Night

Priests, lorry drivers and their wives,
small girls, all asleep in bed.
The café on the square throws
its light onto the pavement.

A white dog barks in the distance.

Orange traffic lights blink.
Behind shuttered windows
the lives, trapped like that dog,
trapped in the darkness.

Morning

Why does he still bother with birdsong, sunrise?
What makes him cling on?
Feeling his stubble, stroking the sheets.

The day shift pull on their uniform. Radiators creak;
freesias are stretching in their vase.

Statistics confirm his best chance is at 4am,
the wolves' hour. That black gap
between the platform and the train.

**Portrait of Johannes Wtenbogaert,
Remonstrant preacher, aged 76**

He stands there and we wonder what he thinks.
His head, resting like a deserted swan
in a nest of fine lace pleats. Did he shrink
even once from God's black skull cap plan?

In a corner, placed to catch the light,
the book we expect is his bible. No,
those pages curling away from top right
are not yet half full, and only we know

this preacher would live till nearly ninety.
Too tired to protest, he faces Rembrandt
who paints a life-like sketch where we can see
the frayed edge of the limp cloth in his hand.

Joan

One of the girls I went to college with
was Joan who'd left home early.

She smoked Gauloises, had a stubborn
streak, wanted to study philosophy.

We thought she was depressed; she cut
herself and once put out a cigarette on her arm.

I wish I'd asked her why. I can see her now
with that hair cropped short, staring straight ahead.

People shouting, the smoke, the crackling fire.
Too hot, I need to step back.

Satsumas

The mandarin is also a clementine, or a seedless tangerine.
They must not be confused with the satsuma, first
exported from the province of Satsuma in Japan.

The men and women of the Fruit-and-Veg Marketing Board
are introducing their successes: the Orkney, a type
of button mushroom, but a clear ice-white and stoic.
There is the Argyle, an improved form of celery with
lower water content, therefore less stringy and greener.
The Devon is already being exported to Japan:
a small tasty apple, dark red, square and stackable.

No-one mentions the Wicklow with a taste like ratatouille
after a fortnight in the fridge, or the Sark, a long, sour,
brown hairy thing lying at the back in wooden crates.

Prelude and fugue

I enter and dare a glance at your effects –
    straight rows of books in alphabetical order
    the white board emptied
    pens and pencils (four of each)
    manuscript paper and a rubber
    on the Yamaha
You were filling in the bass line.

Music for a while shall all your cares beguile.

You kept some organ pipes in the loft.
You were going to build one.
What happened to those when you moved
into the flat?

Sometimes I turned the pages for you
feet darting across the pedals.
When I was twelve I left the choir
and gave up singing.

Your black shoes scuffed at the side.

The Catholics paid best you said:
a bonus for weddings and funerals.

On the beach

Against the sinking sun gulls ride the waves.
Our dogs bark and chase their tails.
Try to run with a lone jogger who braves

the east wind whistling. Your son trails
in your wake, attempts big steps. Laughter peals:
a scene lifted straight from some fairy tale.

Heaped grey boulders mimic a colony of seals.
Not long before love winters in my heart.
I need to tell you how it feels

to be together, yet growing apart.
Your craggy face seems so much older
clouded in a bluish hue. I brace myself to start

as you place a hand on my shoulder
but all I can say is *It's getting colder*.

Mishap

It was all voice-activated
and I didn't know whether
to speak German straight away
or wait till I got to Leipzig.
I'd prepared a list of questions
to ask J S Bach, smuggled
in a cassette recorder
with the fugue my late father
had composed in his honour.

A muddle of digits and dials.
In the adrenalin rush
I wasn't fast enough to decipher
all those Roman numerals.

So, there I was, in the fertile
Nile delta, queuing up to dance
for Amenhotep III, doing that
sideways walk with the hands,
worried Anubis would scorn my heart,
knowing that the time machine
would be appropriated
by Amenhotep for his tomb
and the journey to the afterlife.

The hermit

The hermit had to be retired
for health and safety reasons.

He was flown out of the desert,
given a dictionary and glasses.

He is renting an old longhouse,
leaves doors and windows open

so he can smell the cool air,
but still he cannot sleep.

The postman was his first visitor.
Mail lies piled up by the gate.

The grains of sand on the beach
make him feel homesick even now.

By the light of a candle he may
be able to look in the mirror, but not yet.

Lost

Things get lost in many ways.
Dogs slip their lead.
A waterfall dries up.
A gold ring is thrown away in anger.
The baker swears at the burnt loaves.

More than we can count
and hold in our empty hands
gets lost in time, the silent space.
Horses, kingdoms, forests, cathedrals
disappear in a single minute.

*

The translator sits very still.
She is shifting grains of sand from
one hand into a small glass bowl.
The sand sighs; she only hears
the music in her head.

It: that insignificant word.
The tall, thin *I,* standing for
what doesn't want to be known,
refuses to be found. It turns,
steps away through the mirror.

The small letter *t,* a tongue;
a place for a brief rest
near the end of the journey;
a small gold dagger, trying
to protect all that's ever been lost.

Round and round

Tracing the shape of your brow
with my fingers I fear
the moment you whisper *My dear*.

Always too soon. *I must go now.*
After you've left I envy her
tracing the shape of your brow.

I curl up, straighten the pillow,
commit myself for another year
though I hate it: lying here
tracing the shape of your brow.

From Grassington, June
for Dave Smith

We had been following the Roman road:
Rita who was almost 80,
her bearded son, clutching champagne,
the pale daughter-in-law, and me
still gripping the metal frame.

Our shadow floated ahead of us,
scaring sheep and deer into running
towards the orange early evening.
The only sound creaking wicker
and the hissing of gas.

We ducked as we rushed over
telephone lines, fences, tree tops.
The Land Rover – still keeping up –
with the bottle of whisky to placate
the farmer on whose field we hoped to land.

The ghosts have swapped houses

Just for the summer months
he tells me. *Portugal next year.*
We're in the kitchen.
My Campari soda drew him in.

Spitting blood in a white bowl.

A litany: porcelain, gold, crowns,
bridges, implants, root canals.

Ceiling height aquariums, Botox,
text reminders, I say. He sighs
and squints against the sun.

This room in Samur is spacious,
tranquil, a thin grey layer
rests on the furniture, the corner
cupboards that seem to float.
A chair has been placed by the window.
It is eager, leans forward into the sun.

I point. *Those specks of orangey-red*
at the edges? He nods and smiles:
two unmarried sisters, a quiet life.
Residue of fear; makes me feel at home.

A room in Samur, 1990. Artist: Stephen Farthing,
Sheffield Galleries & Museums Trust.

Flight of swallows, murmuration of starlings

A long line of scarecrows was no defence.
Each day at dusk more words arrived.
Small words with soft downy feathers, large
words that made strange gurgling sounds:
Litany, Lamentation. They roosted
on telegraph wires, fences round his fields.

His wife had been a word collector. She kept
thousands in small paper boxes called books.
These boxes were lined up in coloured rows
in cases, on wooden shelves and tables.
She had taken the books with her when she left
calling him *spineless* and *an empty well.*

His neighbour Charlie, the old lion tamer, came
with his black boots, his long whips. The birds
hissed and pecked at Charlie's hat. Feral words.
He remembered his mother telling him stories
about loaves and fishes, storms of locusts.
The local preacher came in his long black coat.
His booming sermon scared away the clouds.
The words spread their feathers, glinting
in the sun; closed their small fierce eyes.

That night a small red hen walked into his dream.
She had made hundreds of prints in the fresh snow.
The hen stood on a book with his wife's name on it.
The next morning he drove into town, bought the only
poetry book in the remainder shop. A poet who had taught
himself, a goatherd from Orihuela, Miguel Hernández.

Poems of love, loss, war; poems of prison.
Miguel died in prison not yet 32.
The telegraph wires pinged. The words watched.
Your heart is a frozen orange. A bird on the wing
like *a thirsty handkerchief hovers, hoping to drink tears.*
The old farmer, for the first time in his life, crying.

Laughter

The laughter swaying across the lettuce,
strong knotted rope in the old Bramley tree.
A grandmother sits quietly in a wooden chair;
she counts knitting patterns in her head.

The dappled shade is a cool alleyway
between her life and her daughter's world.
Laughter slides away from them, low
down across the grass; it hides
between the rhubarb and redcurrant bushes,
waiting until night time for the moles
to come up and breathe into it.
Yesterday's laughter a small pile of earth.

I want to be

a clown in a travelling circus,
flapping through the ring
in big black, shiny shoes, cry
my crocodile tears, squirting
arcs of water on decent men
in the front row shielding
the small boy they doubt is theirs.

We travel slowly to the next town
and that's when I dream
of being a diplomat or spy.
In a way I am a diplomat
because my falling over
makes them laugh; and I spy
something in them with my big
blue eye, and it may be a truth, or a lie,
but it's always a secret.

On reaching his 102ⁿᵈ birthday

He always liked his drink,
so it's no surprise that Albert went North,
that unused train ticket in his pocket.

He is said to have died in a car crash,
but police do know people who
walk away and without a scratch.

After walking for weeks he reached Norway
where the days are short
and the nights are made for alcohol.

Camus lived in a modest house
with a butcher's block in the kitchen
where he cut reindeer and smoked.

A flock of swans flew through his dreams,
so he married the next woman to walk past,
taught her two sons to play football.

She taught him to sleep soundly at last.
A *pied-noir* at rest under the *Herring Lights,*
on the cold edge of man's world.

Yellowish green and faint red glowing,
these arcs and rays and curtains of gas,
the fight against dawn and the sun.

June rain
for Christopher and Marisa

It's June and the rain is falling.
It is cooler and darker now.
It's the rain we prayed for last night,
though we'd not meant to do such a thing.

The old women, eight or nine, spread
across benches outside the church.
Us along the tables, a line of snails,
sloping down towards the blue house.

It was speaking of Sundays now filled
with shopping and the silence
that binds Quakers together.

And it's in silence we, snails,
all of us with our whorled shells
of stories, sit at the breakfast table.

The cheep-cheep-cheep of birds
after the rain is flowing into the room
and a fresh breeze that tells of new stories.

Festes patronals

float of the Virgin
her lights switched off switched on
as she sways downhill

smiling at Saints Cosmo and Damian
the Rwandan priest

young girls carry
pots of basil on their heads –
the boys' awkward hands

Dios es Amor
pavements streaked with candle wax

last back on the square
the old bachelor
and his Zimmer frame

Grandfather Lutz

He was shy, had a slight stoop.
His grandmother told him to go outside,
get a fresh nose, play like a normal child.

From that grandmother he inherited
the steady eye; the patient, calm hands.

That's how Gutenberg became European
champion, three years running,
in the adult heavyweight marbles.

Later he coached his apprentices
while they waited for the ink to dry.

If Bach had been a baker

If Bach had been a baker, that dozen
buns would now be humming inside the oven.
J.S. stands there and he hums too, he knows
in time each grain, each tiny grain grows.
The job suits his temperament well;
the baker's house is the place to dwell.
Full trays of buns lined up – round notes, a chord.
Each day he rises and gives thanks to the Lord.
His wife is waiting, holds out the clean, fresh
white smock. Then he hugs her, strokes her flesh;
he blows her kisses, steps into the light
where he can raise the flour on left and right.
          Brot und Kuchen:
          Ja, hier gibt es alles was Sie suchen.

Bach *am* Bach: a corner plot by the brook,
the swaying leaded sign a prayer book.
Today, how big and bold the letters glow;
a rainbow-colour Bach with specks of snow.
The steamy windows held so safely in
the brown baguette of brick, next to its twin.
Just now a stork was sighted and it's true:
in nine months' time a son for Bach is due.

Inside the smell of bread brings tears to one's eye
and I can see you now as you still try
to resist, resist Bach's God-blessed fruit loaf:
vanilla, almond, honey, spice and clove.
That thirteenth bun would not have been required
as Bach the baker would have been inspired
by God and luck would not have been his guide.
His name and fame in time go country-wide
and people will come to stand and hear
him hum and sing to flour, to grain; so clear
his voice, so pure the water and the yeast:
our daily bread transformed into a feast.

Eel

I have time now
and feel safe.

I wriggle in the sand,
the sun showering
gold coins onto the riverbed.

At night I dance with otters,
sing duets with the moon.

Another morning will come
when I'm full-grown, turn into prey.

Today the sand is warm.
I'm safe in my skin.

Things I want you to bring when you next visit

Three or four bags of liquorice,
animals or coins, doubly or trebly-salted;
three tins of *Zonnatura* tea,
the one with twenty herbs
that smells of aniseed
when you pull the foil lid;
a yellow double-decker train
slicing through the horizon;
the silhouette of a village church;
and the wide, sandy, shell-scattered beach.

Another life

I didn't know I would be swimming
through water and icy air
with the trees on both sides
of the river green, still, tall,
and blue sky separating them.

I didn't know that trees can swim
and that the birches with their freckled,
fire-blasted bark had been
swans in another life.

I didn't know I would be swimming
among the trees, small green leaves
stroking my thighs, and the curved
white necks of swans,
their orange beaks, jet-black eyes.
Breathing out icy air,
breathing in the warmth of swans.
Swimming is another life.

Oversteps Books Ltd

The Oversteps list includes books by the following poets:

David Grubb, Giles Goodland, Alex Smith, Will Daunt, Patricia Bishop, Christopher Cook, Jan Farquarson, Charles Hadfield, Mandy Pannett, Doris Hulme, James Cole, Helen Kitson, Bill Headdon, Avril Bruton, Marianne Larsen, Anne Lewis-Smith, Mary Maher, Genista Lewes, Miriam Darlington, Anne Born, Glen Phillips, Rebecca Gethin, W H Petty, Melanie Penycate, Andrew Nightingale, Caroline Carver, John Stuart, Rose Cook, Jenny Hope, Hilary Elfick, Anne Stewart, Oz Hardwick, Terry Gifford, Michael Swan, Maggie Butt, Anthony Watts, Joan McGavin, Robert Stein, Graham High, Ross Cogan, Ann Kelley, A C Clarke, Diane Tang, R V Bailey, John Daniel, Alwyn Marriage, Kathleen Kummer, Jean Atkin, Charles Bennett, Elisabeth Rowe, Marie Marshall, Ken Head, Robert Cole, Cora Greenhill, John Torrance, Michael Bayley, Christopher North, Simon Richey, Lynn Roberts, Sue Davies, Mark Totterdell, Michael Thomas, Ann Segrave, Helen Overell, Rose Flint, Denise Bennett, James Turner, Sue Boyle, Jane Spiro, Jennie Osborne, John Daniel, Janet Loverseed, Wendy Klein, Sally Festing, Angela Stoner, Simon Williams, Susan Taylor and Richard Skinner.

For details of all these books, information about Oversteps and up-to-date news, please look at our website and blog:

www.overstepsbooks.com
http://overstepsbooks.wordpress.com